THE MAGICAL NEGRO REVEALS HIS SECRET

GABRIEL GREEN

C&R Press
Conscious & Responsible

Winter Soup Bowl Selection
2019 6th Collection Selection 1 of 1 CB 12

All Rights Reserved

Printed in the United States of America

First Edition
1 2 3 4 5 6 7 8 9

Selections of up to two pages may be reproduced without permissions. To reproduce more than two pages of any one portion of this book write to C&R Press publishers John Gosslee and Andrew Sullivan.

Cover art by Nate Lewis
Interior by Jojo Rita

Copyright ©2019 Gabriel Green

ISBN 978-1-949540-11-6

C&R Press
Conscious & Responsible
crpress.org
Long Live Books!

For special discounted bulk purchases, please contact:
C&R Press sales@crpress.org
To book events, readings, and author signings, please contact: info@crpress.org

THE MAGICAL NEGRO REVEALS HIS SECRET

Table of Contents

My Town//5
A Hood Love Story Ending in Broken Promises//6
Ode to the Dandelion//9
In Defense of JR Smith//11
Ours is the Fury//12
my grandma don't remember my name//14
Imposter Syndrome OR The Magical Negro Reveals His Secret//15
The Return (Part 1)//19
In Response to the Intellectual's Groundbreaking Thesis that Race is a Social Construct//20
What is Dead May Never Die//21
Love Poem//24
Song of the Tro Tro #1//26
The Poet Articulates His Most Sincere Apology for Hurting the Feelings of the Well-Intentioned Older White Gentleman who Thought being a Good Guy Meant Incessantly Apologizing for "Racism"//27
The Return (Part 2)//28
The Poet Reconsiders His Views on Having No Children//29
Wedding Cake//30
The Poet, Upon Hearing of a Space Jam Sequel, Finally Concedes that Lebron is Better//32

for Tiran Marion Burrell
Ars Longa, Vita Brevis

My Town

    After Buddy Wakefield
      After Will Evans

After gentrification has eaten its fill and pulled itself from the table - satisfied

and the auto industry leaves
                and a piston finds prettier gears another town over
                              and a lion outgrows its den

and the millage don't pass
                and the road to success corrodes under the weight of
                    snow
                          ice
                                  salt
                                            tire
                                                      repeat

    and the road cracks and craters into
        a pothole obstacle course that swallows everything
            before they black tar the holes as if nothing ever happened

after the *good* schools get funded
        and the emergency manager gets his cut
                and the textbooks age like cheap wine in chipped
glass

and an autumn son bursts through cracked concrete
                            in search of an escape
                                          in search of home

A Hood Love Story, Ending in Broken Promises

Deal.

Joker/Joker/Deuce/Deuce.
colored joker and two of diamonds are big.
yo ass betta pay attention – ain't no table talk.
no mix dealin
no fancy cuttin
my dude...
count yo cards right, we playin sandbags,
just in case y'all some
ole underbiddin-ass-niggas.
& i'm serious about that table talk shit.
i will
fight
you.

Bid.

Praise to the bonds that last thirteen cards at a time
and hands that hold few promises
but a world of possibilities,
where maybe today,
 a king kneels to the pauper.
And maybe a lowly, unassuming soul -
strolling this concrete jungle,
where we cut the hood into the spaded shape
of a block party when the clubs shut down
after three Jack's were found posted up on the corner,
the same corner that sharpens its teeth on diamonds
and swallows beating hearts whole -
maybe tonight,
that soul
skates.

Play.

Partner, how many books you got?

               i got two and a
               STRONG
               possible.

i'm thinkin board.

*i got four, fa sho i might
can make some miracles
happen*

               *play yo hand,
               fuck what they
               talkin bout.*

               i trust you

---

shit! who dealt this hand?!

this a misdeal

               what?!

*man, i told you these
some under-biddin-ass niggas.*

               *i count eight, shiiiid
               y'all might as well
               bid a boston.*

*bruh, my hand
bleeding over here.*

Board.

Tonight, I place the fate of my glory and the power of my undoing in your hands. I've shared many tables, indulged in some of the greatest feast a backyard has to offer, broken bread with friends and strangers and new friends. I've built castles fifty-two fickle bricks at a time and seen what happens when the perfect storm lays claim to it. I believe nothing to be permanent. Nothing built with these hands meant to last beyond the next fateful wind. I know my value depends not on what I bring to the table, but what I build upon pulling my chair up. I know I have no say in the tools with which I build. But my grandfather once said, give me a screwdriver and a hammer and I will build you a home. My hands hold no miracles but magic rests in my fingertips. So tonight, as the sun drinks its last fill of sky, drooping gracefully into a soft lavender and orchid cloud, I memorize your face, reread the stories behind your eyes, take mental pictures of every fault line and contour of your cheekbones. You do the same. And we rehearse the language of unspoken joy, fear, anticipation, sorrow, assurance, uneasiness, hope. And you make a silent vow that if it ever becomes necessary, the dreadful cutting of nose to spite face – to still find me, beautiful.

Set.

my nigga!
did you just renege?

Ode to the Dandelion

And ain't that like a rose?

Always getting what she wants.
The uninvited belle of the ball,
rearing her gorgeous head,
all prickly, pretty, pitiful, painful, n'shit,
to lay claim to every eye and heart.

And ain't that like a rose?

Colonizer of urban soil, taking up space,
here to gentrify the concrete forest.
The ally that want all the attention,
want all the credit for finding rich soil
under cement desert.

And what of the dandelion?

The flower the rest of the garden
will call a weed behind its back.
What of the roots that swim through cracked granite,
and stand under the stampede of poets
who marvel and beat their quills into fettered vanes
writing of privileged roses
but ignoring the coalescent bouquet
of "find-a-way-or-make-one"?

What of the dandelion
who dares dream in the face of death,
and under gentlest breeze,
blow a diaspora
of wishes
for an offspring's better inheritance?

Staring down the eye of a nozzle
awaiting chemical warfare, at best
or the violent plucking from home, at worst
to make room for the good grass
yet still have the audacity to mimic
the sun's shine?

In Defense of JR Smith

And who among you, has not been caught unaware of the score? Who among you, has not dared dream so big as to believe yourself victor, in a game the experts called for the other team before you ever arrived? Forget about the stacked odds that suggested you never had a chance to begin with. Forget about the prevailing narrative that you ain't shit. Never been shit. Ain't never gon be shit. Forget that your very presence here is borrowed time against the inevitable. Who hasn't held joy in their fingertips long enough to memorize its texture, before fate cruelly reminds you that that joy wasn't yours? That it was never meant for you in the first place? Who hasn't figured the shape of glory spherical, and a single flick's rotation away from spinning toward your will?

What is victory for the {always} jest? Triumph for the {always} foil? Punchline to the joke that stopped being funny the first time it was uttered? Sure, your opponent is always "better". And you ain't even supposed to be here. But, how many of you could awaken to tune of your greatest failure being played on repeat, and in the face of amused pity and contempt, suit up for the next game?

Ours is the Fury

Son,
I know you mad.
I know what it means
to have a fire trapped within your pupils,
embers that singe through corneas,
burning a trail to your brain,
through your nervous system,
creating a dry forest of your limbs.
The spark of steel
and the wind of another body hitting the ground
threatening to set your body ablaze.

I know what rage looks like.

I've seen it before.

Back in '92,
when they beat a man half to death, on camera,
and called it a Wednesday.
I felt a barrel of wild fire
explode in my chest.
How else do you explain the feeling
of being told whether or not your body
is compliant or not,
if it is breathing, it is a danger
that must be cut at its source?
I never wanted so badly to kill with my bare hands.
But,
in those hands was a note
from your mother.
We needed eggs, milk, and meat.
And you needed a father
to teach you to cook one day.
Besides,

I'd known what rage looked like.

I'd seen it before.

Back in '68,
when they killed a King's cries for justice
and I watched flames engulf a city
one block at a time.
My mother and I watched
on our front porch,
as a dream became deferred,
and dried under a summer sun,
and the winds shouted
a sorrowful cry
for vengeance.
And friction from the limbs of
leftover marches
sparked a raging fire in the street.
We watched it burn.
No tears.
Besides,

We'd seen this before.

Son,
I've lived through enough fires,
brushed off years of ashes to know
ain't but two ways to exist here:
Live long enough to warn your sons of
the fire they inherited, and how to live with it
or
let the fire consume you, scorch the earth,
and hope the flames burn it all to dust.

my grandma don't remember my name

it sits like a phantom touch on the brain
the same way a dream rests at the edge of a recollection she knows
she's seen before, tries her hardest to grasp whatever still dangles
from her mind's cliff.

my name is become
the forgotten melody i convince myself
she is trying to sing whenever i hear her hummed wailing.
it used to be a full song.

but if i try hard enough
i can hear her playing it
on her old out-of-tune piano whose notes
always seemed to bend and behave to her voice.

both her hands and voice are brittle now.

Imposter Syndrome OR The Magical Negro Reveals His Secret

To begin,
you should probably know that nothing
I tell you is a lie. Certainly not one
solitary Truth, but definitely honest
to the best of my knowledge.
It starts –
like all magic –
with a slight of hand, misdirection
from one viewpoint to distract from
the trick being performed right
in front of your very eyes.

Watch closely. Now,

hold in your mind, the image
of a stained glass self-portrait
which contains the magician's True likeness.
Now let it go.
Watch it fall to the ground
shattering into a million pieces.
Remember this image for later.

*****

If I were to tell you that
I was, in fact, a broken

man, the mistake would be

to assume something went terribly wrong
or that I am in need of your

assistance, though I'd never hold

that against you. Words are sometimes
tricky to get a handle on.

*****

An imposter is someone who assumes
false identities in order to deceive

himself.

But surely, you know the difference between
 mirrors and the objects they reflect.

The mistake would be to assume

a smoke-filled hall of mirrors
 playing some dishonest trick on your eyes.

Remember the image.

*****

My advisor tells me that maybe
the ancient Greek philosophers
got it wrong, hustling backwards
looking for an objective Truth.
*Protagoras was mah dude. 'Man is the
measure of all things'. Later for
allat 'absolute Truth' bullshit.*
I'm inclined to believe him.
Cold to you might be hot
to me, might be just right to
the next person. We can't all be
wrong, surely. Only way to know
for sure is to step outside and
feel for ya self.

Now them Greeks was prolly onto something
with that whole tripartite soul concept.
Or at least the division into threes.
For some reason, we humans love ourselves

some threes. Don't worry. I won't
belabor you with all the different
iteration of threes we can't seem
to get enough of. I just imagine
it's a lot easier to organize the endless
pieces of that which makes up the world.
A tripartite identity. Seems cool enough.

*****

Imposter syndrome is the fear that
one's accomplishments are not

of their own doing, and the subsequent fear

of being exposed as a fraud.
The mistake would be to assume

I've accomplished anything. The greater

mistake is to assume I didn't
arrange it this way from the beginning.

*****

My advisor (who I should add is
a far greater magician than myself, or
else why would he be my advisor?)
tells me that the problem with most
black folk in the academy is that we're too
talented. *Too many things you're
good at, dividing ya attention
from that scholarship.*
Again, I'm inclined to agree.
A triple-threat is child's play over here.
I'm the best poet/scholar/bass player/
singer/chef/hooper/sports aficionado/
jazz historian/Game of Thrones expert I know.

Don't believe me? I invite you
to come find out. You might call it
"Jack of all trades, master of none."

You'd be wrong.

*****

The mistake is to assume mastery
was ever the goal. The greater mistake
is to assume I ever intended you see
the whole Truth. Is it ever not
a matter of misdirection?
A question of perspective?
A matter of proximity and illusion?
For God's sake, remember the image.

a shattered glass image
                of the magician's True likeness
                              viewed from the intimate vantage point
                                        of a single shard.

get it?

The Return (Part 1)

This time
I walked onto the vessel
voluntarily.
No assembly line of sorrow
or blunt stick jabbing flesh forward;
bodies stripped under baking sun.
No chains choking skin
step by bloody step
out of doors we would never see again.

This time
the voyage through death reversed course,
east by day *and* by night
from hell, home.
Vessel got room enough
for everybody. The cargo
ain't got a village wondering
what happened to it.
I got my own seat.
It's comfortable.

Nobody wanna throw themselves
overboard. The ocean looks better
from this angle. The moon's face
glides over peaceful waters.
I sleep, easy.
The sun greet me by the name
I was given, in a language
I don't understand.
All veils removed
Tongue dipped in Twi.

In Response to the Intellectual's Groundbreaking Thesis that Race is a Social Construct

And of course
I am aware of the biblical advice
not to build one's house
upon sand.
I imagine that sand had a past somewhere
way back when
it was more than the butt end
of a parable.
But what, I ask you,
is sand except the remains
of rocks rubbing each other
the wrong way?
And who am I,
but another body rubbed raw,
washed upon a shore full
of beach houses
constructed from palm tree bark
held together by wet
then sunbaked sand bricks?
What you call an imaginary
shelter, I call a childhood.
My house is about as constructed
as time, and according to my watch,
another hurricane is on the horizon.
And my view of the sun –
an arm's length away from
an ocean that can't decide
between swallowing me whole and
spitting my bones
onto the shore or
dragging my body out
further with each tide
to never be seen again –
looks a helluva lot better from
my bedroom window.

What is Dead May Never Die

But rises again, harder and stronger.
And aren't we a blessed people,
bestowed salt, and steel, and stone turned soot?
Are we not a godly host;
the seed of Lodos,
walking into the mouth of a rising tide
to be swallowed,
take council with the Drowned God
and await our promised resurrection?

And one day, fifteen bodies washed up upon the shore.
Their bodies bloated,
column bound together by seaweed.
And a salt sea poured from our eyes
As we made prayers to the drowned god.

Say the words.

What is dead may never die.
But rises again, harder and stronger.

And one day, thirteen more bodies washed up upon the shore.
Their bodies, bloated;
soldiers, said to be too far inland
to be under protection for goods bought with the iron price.
And a salt sea poured from our eyes
as we amended two prayers to the drowned god.

Say
the words.

What is dead may never die.
But rises again, harder and stronger.

And one day, twelve more bodies washed upon the shore
in the dark of night

followed by twenty-seven children;
a baptism gone wrong.
Their bodies, bloated.
And we made ornaments of their bones,
blamed the amount of blood
on the jagged {isolated} rocks in the harbor,
said *we cannot legislate every stone,*
our forbearers placed them there for our protection
and it is blasphemy to question the will
of the drowned god.
And from our eyes a flood of salt water
engulfed the bodies,
whole.
Washing away everything
but
their names.

You <u>know</u> the words.

What is dead may never die.
But rises again, harder and stronger.

And one day, thirty-two more bodies
washed up upon the shore,
and fifty more,
and twenty-seven more,
and fifty-nine more,
and seventeen more,
and eleven more,
and fifty more,
and their bodies, bloated,
billowing a watery accusation
of a drunken, drowned god
who had grown fat off their bodies
gorging himself on their insides.
His mouth too full, spitting them onto
the shore.

But we can't call god a murderer.
Water is that which cleanses,
purifies.
And our eyes monsoon a salt ocean
to wash all life.

Drink the words.

What   dead
         rises   again?
                         Die
             again, harder   stronger.

Love Poem
(Fragment from Donald Trump's Inaugural Address)

thank you.
We
are now joined in a

promise
Together,
for years to come.

We will face challenges. We will confront hardships. But we will get the job done.

we gather
power, and we are

magnificent.

Today
today
i   A m

giving   you, the
              reaped   rewards of

triumph

celebrate
              right here, and right now,
this moment

I belong to

you ▇ .

What truly matters

will be forgotten no longer.

hear these words:
You will never be ignored again.
Your voice
will define our   destiny.
And your   love will
forever guide us   .

Together, We   Strong   .

We   Proud   .
We   Safe   .
And, Yes,
Together,
We   Great   .

Song of the Tro Tro #1
(Ghanaian Sun Plays the Dozens with American Boy)

Yo deodorant is a baaaaad ally.
It stank. With all its good intentions,
doin none of the work
but want all the attention.

Wants every soul, sardined into
this seven passenger van that maxed out
in capacity about eight people ago
to know it's down with the struggle.

Yo sweat just Deebo'd yo armpits.
                              {WHAT deodorant?!?!}

Yo sweat asked to see a manager.
Said it paid too much money
to be evicted from skin
for no reason other than, "it's hot".

Yo forehead look like moist double-consciousness.
Ole cognitive dissonance head ass.
Veil all salty, soaked, and translucent,
resting hot and sticky against skin.

Yo sweat is privilege leaving the body,
and yo shirt is drenched.
The origins of which you also
don't know, but you wear it anyway –

like the skin you couldn't identify
if it called you by name,
but you be ready to fight the fool
who'd dare challenge your ownership of it.

The Poet Articulates His Most Sincere Apology for Hurting the Feelings of the Well-Intentioned Older White Gentleman who Thought being a Good Guy Meant Incessantly Apologizing for "Racism"

...
My Bad

The Return (Part 2)

Where are you from?
A broken timeline with a slick tongue.
Can't write its own name in the dirt
but can whisper a lineage through endless
fields, house it within the notes of an old song,
pierce it through aching wails from
flesh ripped by lash, chains crafting a cadence
with each pained step
on piss and blood soaked wood.

No.
Where are you from?
A purgatory where the limbo isn't
the vertical distance between heaven and hell
but the limb tearing pull between two fiery pits.
Where the demons on both sides know me by name
but would rather identify me by the taste
of my bones between their teeth.

No.
Where are you from?
A heart excavated slowly from chest,
bleached, burned, and dried under
southern sun, shattered into
a million pieces, rebuilt and shattered once more.
It makes a ritual of collecting the shards
planting them deep in foreign earth
hoping to reep roots.

No.
Where are you from?
A mother whose face I've never seen.
Voice I've never heard, but chants softly in my ears

Akwaaba
                    Akwaaba
                                      Akwaaba

The Poet Reconsiders His Views on Having No Children

The morning after police unload a clip of fears into a black body until it oozes a bedtime story that never ends, but is stuck in a continuous loop; & after I spend the night in a hotel bed, body curled into a question mark, cursing God for this body that seems only to be read as [caps lock] & [shift 1], a loud exclamation in need of silencing; & after I wake up to a sun with no recollection of the sons burned out in its absence, I find myself in the breakfast buffet, grateful for another day above dirt, if only to experience the gourmet cuisine that is powdered eggs & absurdly cheap bacon. & that's when I see him: black boy, all [caps lock] & [shift 1], wandering the small lobby chanting, *eggs & bacon, eggs & bacon, eggs & bacon*. & nothing carries more importance, more urgency, more heeding attention than this black boy & his quest for breakfast. Our eyes meet, & I remember what it means to be without care or rules about decorum, or speaking too loudly, or wandering so freely. & If only for a moment, the only things that matter are *eggs & bacon*.

Wedding Cake
Lamentation for Byron Douglas III

It's a rather funny notion - *All's fair...*
in terms of what gets caught
within the sticky, suffocating batter
of *everything*. Not necessarily funny
in the sense of a joke shared amongst
lovers, and throngs of friends who've long
known the punch line but laugh anyway.
But rather, funny in the same sense
of the joke a wooden wall tells
an elbow upon hasty encounter
and makes a cracked wedding bell
of the arm, the vibrations singing
a wrenching chord through the limbs
that seems to resonate forever.
I suppose *forever* is kinda funny also.
Like how the heart's gaze is often set
on a finish line we can never see,
yet that blindness is the source of great
comfort. No one ever asks
where forever begins, or how finite creatures
like ourselves even get there.
Yes, I'd sorely want to believe
that we'd last longer than, say
cake does, when abandoned in open
air. I want to believe our composition
able to retain its moisture, even
in the midst of not so subtle breezes
from cars driving off into our promised
sunsets, instead of becoming a dry,
brittle thing, holding on to pockets
of air left behind long after the cheers subside
and the custodial crew finishes sweeping
up fallen pink and white flower petals.
I want to say that you deserved better.
But who ever weeps
for the discarded slice of cake
left to crumble on the table?

The Poet, Upon Hearing of a Space Jam Sequel, Finally Concedes that Lebron is Better

At least there's always '98,
they can't take that away from you.
Skinny black boy all of nine years old (going on ten),
watching the greatest swan to ever
swoon, sing one last song[1]. And oh!
what a tune. Blaring out the solo
of all solos, while the most ironic
franchise name in the history of spor
ts
threatens to ensemble a foil to the only
measure of perfection you'll grow to care about.

And you watch, beating heart in sweaty
hands, as *His Airness* pulls another miracle
out of the small space your imagination
convinced you was his home and his alone.

I mean, really. When's the last time
your idol baptized
an alien in mid-air?— I'll wait.

He catches the inbound at half-court
with just enough burst left in 35 year-old calves
to blow by Byron Russell for the easy
lay-in. Down by one. Back on defense where
the Mailman has the audacity
to ignore *his* presence - mortal fool.

"Double on Malone.
They steal it!"

Time don't stand still, but for *him*,
slows just enough for destiny to beg
one   last   dance.
Bob Costas with the call.

"Jordan......Open......
CHICAGO WITH THE LEAD!!"

---
1   Because of course, no real Jordan fan counts the Wizard years.

*****

Even with hands as small as yours,
there's nothing, in your mind, that can't
be held onto forever.
After all, *he*, armed with nothing more
than a bottle of Gatorade, McDonald's fries,
(and the shoes, gotta be the shoes),
made you believe that man could indeed fly,
that the "physically impossible" was merely a 38 point CV line,
that invincibility could always win the battle
of attrition waged against time in one single body.

And you will stubbornly fight off
the existential crisis that comes with
watching heroes embrace loss, letting go
with little more than a shrugged shoulder
and the phrase, *"It's just........."*

Kinda funny, right?
How four letters
can make the weight of anything
one loves and cares about evaporate
into an opaque nothingness that grasping
fingers can't justify holding on to?

"It's just a game"
will eventually turn **hours** of practicing fadeaway
jumpers (kicked foot, MJ tongue out)
in your cousin's backyard stadium
into the throwaway move you resort
to during Sunday ball at the rec building,
even though "conventional" knowledge
been told you to jack up the 3 instead.

*****

Nine-year-old you will eventually get good at letting
go; twenty years later and a week shy
of thirty — your calves conversing loudly
about this morning's run (as if you can't hear them),
then laughing hysterically at your insistence
to yet dream of 'gettin up and puttin one down',
doubled over at your audacity to double down
on a losing battle with time - *mortal fool.*

Then you'll remember *him*. Free from
the crossover you'll never publicly admit
was a push-off, arm extended, flicked wrist,
dangling fingertips loosely gripping a legacy
long enough to see {swish} hush crowd
before letting   go, and trotting back down the floor.

ACKNOWLEDGEMENTS

By any true and honest measurement, the lineage of grace that make this manuscript possible is both long and comprised of beautiful souls who deserve a full articulation of their contribution. Unfortunately, such an articulation would surely be longer than the manuscript itself. Therefore, I humbly ask the forgiveness of, and extend my deepest thanks to the following:

First and foremost, the Creator who was/is/will be the Muse above of all muses.

The Fam: Solomon and Peggy Green, Siblings: Aaron (Martel) and William, and my extraordinarily large extended family.

Editors of C&R Press, Readers/Judges and fellow poets in the 2019 Winter Soup Bowl competition.

Literary Journals *WusGood?*, *The Amistad*, and *Peregrine* for publication of the following poems: "Ode to the Dandelion", "The Poet Reconsiders His Views On...", "Song of the TroTro #1", & "In Response to the Intellectual's Groundbreaking Thesis..."

The Mentors: Omari "King Wise" Barksdale, Natasha "T. Miller", Scott Woods, William Evans, John "JG the Jugganaut" Gibson, Dr. Keith Gilyard, Dr. Shara McCallum, Dr. Julia Kasdorf

The Poets, (Contemporaries and Influences): Marsha Watson, Chris "Untitled" Jones, Deonte Osayonde, Justin Rodgers, Devin Samuels, Lindsay Stone, Garret Porter, Jamie Morgan-Valenzuela, Tariq Luthun, EMU Poetry Society (WHO R WE?!), Tiran Burrell, Nadine Marshall, Darius Simpson, Krystal Bush, Keith Paul Jason, PSU W.O.R.D.S (What You Got?!), Rabiyatu Jalloh, David Gaines, Davon Clark, Abby Kennedy, Ka'Lee Strawbridge, Kelly Chu, Nadia Souada, Fatimah Ally, Nicole Telfer, Cleo Roseboro, Lara Talal, Asia Bryant-Wilkerson, Seckin Kara, Andrea Brown, Audrey Gradzewicz, Lark Wilson, Jordan McGhee, Laura Nejako, Danielle Ryle, Elizabeth Hopta, Lauren Barron, Erin Servey, Kylie McCool, Katrina Eckel, Kerong Chen, Carolyn Meehan,

Lada Kolomiyets, Alexa Patrick and Julian Randall (CUPSI OG's and Henny compatriots), Hanif Abdurraqib, Siaara Freeman, Britteney "Black Rose" Kapri, Billy Tuggle, Danez Smith, Bernard Ferguson, Jesse Parent, Teresa Siagatonu, Rachel McKibbens, Paul Tran, & and so many more!

The Support System: Daphney Chancy, Dr. Mudiwa Pettus, Shavonte Mills, Brandon Erby, D'Angelo Bridges, Dr. Earl Brooks, Curry Kennedy and Eduardo Ramos (The 'Beership'), Melita Grimes, Anna Bobo, Anthony Cox Jr., Dr. Emil & Tiffany Cunningham, Jonathan Dumas, Charles Gibson, Kameran Davis, Dr. Alphonso Grant, Desvan Moody, Durrell Burns, Mario Martinez, Malcolm Levy, Jahmaad Harrell, & a larger host of friends too wide to justly account for!!

Sincerely,
Gabriel Green
(aka #MusicianPoetScholar, aka 'Magical Negro in Training')

C&R PRESS CHAPBOOKS

C&R Press hosts two chapbook selection periods from June to September and November to March coupled with a reading in New York City each year. The Winter Soup Bowl and Summer Tide Pool Chapbook Series are open to new and established writers in poetry, fiction, essay and other creative writing.

2019 Summer Tide Pool
The Magical Negro Reveals His Secret by Gabriel Green

2018 Winter Soup Bowl
Paleotemptestology by Bertha Crombet
White Boys from Hell by Jeffrey Skinner

2017 Summer Tide Pool
Atypical Cells of Undetermined Significance by Brenna Womer

2017 Winter Soup Bowl
Heredity and Other Inventions by Sharona Muir
On Inaccuracy by Joe Manning

2016 Summer Tide Pool
Cuntstruck by Kate Northrop
Relief Map by Erin M. Bertram
Love Undefined by Jonathan Katz

2016 Winter Soup Bowl
Notes from the Negro Side of the Moon by Earl Braggs
A Hunger Called Music: A Verse History in Black Music by Meredith Nnoka

C&R PRESS TITLES

NONFICTION

Women in the Literary Landscape by Doris Weatherford, et al
Credo: An Anthology of Manifestos & Sourcebook for Creative Writing by Rita Banerjee and Diana Norma Szokolyai

FICTION

Last Tower to Heaven by Jacob Paul
No Good, Very Bad Asian by Lelund Cheuk
Surrendering Appomattox by Jacob M. Appel
Made by Mary by Laura Catherine Brown
Ivy vs. Dogg by Brian Leung
While You Were Gone by Sybil Baker
Cloud Diary by Steve Mitchell
Spectrum by Martin Ott
That Man in Our Lives by Xu Xi

SHORT FICTION

Notes From the Mother Tongue by An Tran
The Protester Has Been Released by Janet Sarbanes

ESSAY AND CREATIVE NONFICTION

In the Room of Persistent Sorry by Kristina Marie Darling
the internet is for real by Chris Campanioni
Immigration Essays by Sybil Baker
Je suis l'autre: Essays and Interrogations by Kristina Marie Darling
Death of Art by Chris Campanioni

POETRY

What Need Have We for Such as We by Amanda Auerbach
A Family Is a House by Dustin Pearson
The Miracles by Amy Lemmon
Banjo's Inside Coyote by Kelli Allen
Objects in Motion by Jonathan Katz
My Stunt Double by Travis Denton
Lessons in Camoflauge by Martin Ott
Millennial Roost by Dustin Pearson
Dark Horse by Kristina Marie Darling
All My Heroes are Broke by Ariel Francisco
Holdfast by Christian Anton Gerard
Ex Domestica by E.G. Cunningham
Like Lesser Gods by Bruce McEver
Notes from the Negro Side of the Moon by Earl Braggs
Imagine Not Drowning by Kelli Allen
Notes to the Beloved by Michelle Bitting
Free Boat: Collected Lies and Love Poems by John Reed
Les Fauves by Barbara Crooker
Tall as You are Tall Between Them by Annie Christain
The Couple Who Fell to Earth by Michelle Bitting
Notes to the Beloved by Michelle Bitting

www.ingramcontent.com/pod-product-compliance
Lightning Source LLC
Chambersburg PA
CBHW032106040426
42449CB00007B/1201